POSY
EDWARDS

miley cyrus
Annual 2011

Introduction

It's hardly possible, even if you've been living under a rock for the past few years, that you won't have heard of the global singing sensation that is Miley Cyrus. She rocketed to fame as the tween living the dream double life of popstar and ordinary schoolgirl in the TV show *Hannah Montana*. Since the show's huge success, Miley has stunned everyone with her talents – she has now starred in four seasons and a feature film of *Hannah Montana*, sold millions of albums, played to sold-out crowds in stadiums across the world, and kept her trademark smile on her face all the time too!

Even though, sadly, the fourth series of *Hannah Montana* is set to be the final series, this sassy Tennessee-born teen has plenty of other projects she's keeping busy with, like feature films and new albums, so we know there will be plenty more of Miley to come. Phew!

But one of the most admirable things about Miley is how, despite being an international megastar, she has stayed true to herself and her fans. Just how does this incredibly talented girl keep herself grounded, and not let it go to her head? What's her favourite ice cream flavour? Which *Hannah Montana* star are you most similar to? And just how can you make your very own Miley-inspired glitter jewellery? Read on, for all these fun things and more!

Meet Miley!

Miley Cyrus was born in Franklin, Tennessee in 1992 – but she didn't come into this world as a Miley. When she was born, her given name was in fact Destiny Hope Cyrus. Her father – famous country singer, Billy Ray Cyrus – always knew it was her destiny to bring hope to the world, which was how she got her name. But the bubbly little girl was always so happy and upbeat that she was nicknamed 'Smiley' by her family! That was shortened to Miley in time, so back in 2008 Miley officially changed her name from Destiny Hope Cyrus to Miley Ray Cyrus – taking the same middle name as her famous dad, awww!

Child Star

As a child, Miley was always interested in performing – taking after dad, Billy Ray. When she was nine, she started taking acting classes, and won a few small roles on TV. Sometimes she even hijacked her dad's shows! Miley says, 'I would go on tour with him, and my dad says I would escape from the nanny and run out on stage and have my own little show!' Miley's godmother – the country singing star Dolly Parton – told Miley to sign with a talent management agency, which she did, and it wasn't long before she heard about a role that got her really excited. It was for a Disney series based around a young girl who lived a secret life as a popstar, while going to a high school and pretending to be an ordinary girl – the best of both worlds. No wonder she was excited! How cool!

Audition Limbo

When Miley was in sixth grade, every minute she wasn't studying, she was auditioning for tv shows in LA. It was a tiring lifestyle – balancing her quest to be on TV with her school work. But the hard work paid off when she was eleven and she got a phonecall from Disney asking her to audition for the TV show we now know as *Hannah Montana*. Initially, Miley auditioned for the part of Lilly, the best friend of the lead character. The executives at Disney thought that Miley was too young – and too small – to act in the show. But she was so desperate for the part that eventually they called her back in for more auditions. Impressed with the small Southern girl's big voice and big talent, in the end they cast her in the lead role. Not bad, when you consider that over 1000 hopeful actresses wanted that same part! Soon after that, Miley had to audition her own father for the role of Miley Stewart's father in the show! It's a good job he passed the audition, or who knows what might have happened!

THINGS YOU DIDN'T KNOW ABOUT MILEY.

Miley attends church regularly with her family, and says that her faith is a big part of her life.

Miley Factfile

Date of birth:
23 November 1992

Place of birth:
Franklin, Tennessee, USA

Birth Name:
Destiny Hope Cyrus

Nicknames:
Smiley, Miley, Miles

Height:
5' 4" (1.64 m)

Family:
Miley's Mom and Dad are Tish Cyrus and
Billy Ray Cyrus. Miley has five siblings: older brothers Christopher Cody and Trace Cyrus, older sister Brandi Cyrus, and
younger siblings Braison Cyrus and Noah Lindsey Cyrus

Favourite sports:
Cheerleading, horse riding

Favourite foods:
Chinese food, Pringles, ice cream – yum!

Favourite hobby:
Going shopping, of course!

Favourite season:
Summer

Favourite colours:
Pink, Green and Purple, oh, and more pink!

Pets:
Miley has four dogs, Loco (who is crazy), Juicy (named after the clothing brand), Minnie Pearl and her newest pup, a German shepherd called Mate. How cute!

Favourite outdoor activities:
Running and biking

Favourite actresses:
Miley is a huge fan of Angelina Jolie, Jennifer Aniston, Meryl Streep and Jodie Foster

Favourite candy:
Starburst, Gummy Bears, Peach Rings and Dots

Favourite clothing stores:
Nordstrom and Hollister

Worst habit:
Biting her nails, eew!

Favourite breakfast food:
Lucky Charms or a bowl of oatmeal with two scoops of ice cream

Guitar Star!

Do you want to be a popstar like Miley? Ever dreamed of playing the guitar? If so, you'll need to customise your own superstar guitar to make it completely unique. Use pens, glitter, foil and get creative! Miley likes hers to be pink and sparkly!

Hannah Montana

– Music's Biggest Star is the School's Biggest Secret!

Having won the part of Miley Stewart – and with dad Billy Ray safely on board – Miley and the rest of the cast set about making the Disney series that would catapult them all to world stardom!

The storyline of the series was set around central character, Miley Stewart, who had just moved to Malibu from Tennessee, with her father Robbie Ray and her older brother, Jackson. Even though Miley seems like your average girl, she's hiding a huge secret – she's actually the famous pop star, Hannah Montana! Her best friends at her new school, Lilly Truscott and Oliver Oken, both find out about her big secret, but they manage to keep it to themselves, while also dealing with the every day problems that lots of teenagers have to face: bullies at school, pimples, an evil cousin, and boyfriend troubles.

Curtain's Up!

On 24th March 2006, the long wait was finally over and Hannah Montana was aired on the Disney Channel for the very first time and boy did it pull in the viewers! 5.4 million people across the world tuned in to witness one of the most hotly anticipated TV shows of all time! Within a few weeks, Miley had gone from home-town girl to international superstar! Here's the low-down on what has happened so far!

Hannah Montana Season One

We meet Miley for the first time and she is desperately trying to keep her secret superstar alter ego under wraps. But, she realises it is tough keeping secrets from your BFF so she shares her secret with BFF Lilly and Oliver. Her new celebrity lifestyle takes a bit of getting used to and she doesn't always manage to keep her cool, but it shows Miley that while all the perks she gets as a celeb, her friends mean the world to her.

We also meet 'frenemies' Amber, Ashley and Rico. And who could forget the first time Jake Ryan comes to school …

What's your favourite episode from Season One?

Hannah Montana Season Two

A little bit older and wiser now, Miley starts school again and is starting to cope with the eternal balancing act of superstar Hannah and everyday Miley. Jake comes back and again Miley faces the dilemma – should she tell Jake? What would you do?

We also meet Mikayla this season who turns out to be Miley's new rival and let's not forget Rico who seems to be making a nuisance of himself at every turn!

And with *Hannah Montana* becoming one of the hottest shows on TV, everyone wants to get in on the act. In Season Two guest stars include the Jonas Brothers and Jesse McCartney. Swoon!

Hannah Montana Season Three

In Season Three we see Miley and her friends and frenemies really grow up and take on more responsibility in their lives, though they find out that sometimes they maybe don't want it just yet … tell us about it!

Miley takes the big step of trying to get her driver's licence, which leads to some major embarrassment! Miley also gets her own bank account to let her spend her own money – just think of how many shoes she could buy!

It's clear that Miley is now smarter, sharper and more grown up than we've ever seen her before!

Hannah Montana Season Four

Boooo … Sadly, Season Four is the last season of *Hannah Montana,* and we don't want to spoil it for you. Why not organise a sleepover for the last episode and throw your very own *Hannah Montana* party?

Hannah Montana The Movie

Given that the whole world was going Miley mad, the next step was to make the *Hannah Montana* movie. As her dad says, 'she loves acting, she loves singing, and she loves writing songs.' Wow, she really is one talented girl! In the film, Hannah Montana starts to get a bit big for her boots and is threatening to take over Miley's normal life, so her dad decides to get things under control and hauls her out of the Hollywood highlife and back to her wholesome Tennessee roots. Back in Tennessee, Miley falls for an old flame, Travis, and patches up her friendship with Lilly, despite finding it difficult readjusting to farm life. When Travis catches Miley with her Hannah Montana wig in her hand, he rejects her but, in the end, his respect for Miley brings him back to support her. Awww! And Miley's faith in the best of both worlds is restored! Hannah Montana and Miley – respect in equal parts.

'It is important to remember that I am a real person, have feelings and all that crazy stuff. I think this movie is really going to prove that to people. It all is real, ' says Miley

Although many teenagers might have found it weird working with their dads, Miley couldn't have been happier. 'This may sound weird coming from a teenager, but I like when my dad gets a little frustrated with me or a little upset with me,' she says. 'There aren't a lot of dads like that in this business. Most parents with kids in the business are like "Go free, do what you want". My parents never wanted me to go all Hollywood. My mom's dad died when she was 18, and if anything ever happened to one of my parents, I'd want them to go knowing that I made them proud.'

The Only Way Is Up!

Though the past four years of *Hannah Montana* have brought so much joy to Hannah fans across the world, sadly, Disney decided after Series Four it was time to bring the show to an end. But with new albums and feature films already in the pipeline – watch out for Miley starring in big screen movies *Wings*, *LOL* and *Wake* – one thing's for sure, no more Hannah won't mean the end of the real star of the show, Miley Cyrus! Phew! *Wings* is based on a series of four books by Aprilynne Pike and the main character Laurel discovers she is a fairy.

'As soon as I read the script (For Hannah Montana), I knew it kinda related to me. I wanted to disguise myself as not some celebrity's daughter, just be me and find people that like me for me.'

Make Your Own HANNAH MONTANA Glitter Jewellery

Want your accessories to sparkle and shine just like Miley's? Why not make yourself an amazing glitter necklace and bracelet set, to really make you stand out from the crowd! Hippy bead necklaces are really coming back into fashion, and Miley loves wearing them. This is a super easy way to make your own!

WARNING: this activity is messy, so make sure you ask an adult to help you put down newspaper or a waterproof tablecloth before you begin.

You will need

Newspaper
Scissors
String
A box of cocktail sticks
Colour glitter
Colour paints

Wallpaper paste, or you can make your own glue by mixing one cup of flour with one cup of water and mixing to a smooth paste
Clear nail varnish

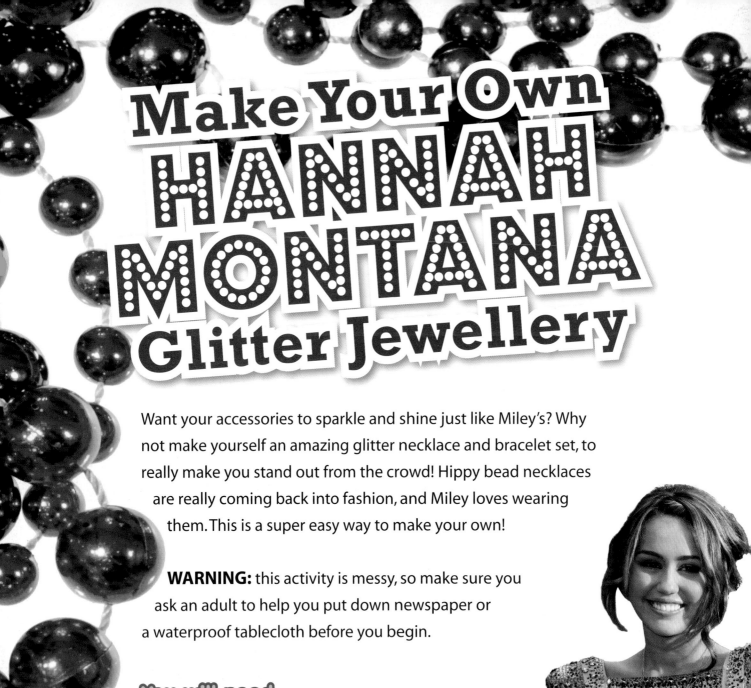

Step 1 Cut the newspaper into long thin strips, between 1-2cm wide, depending on how big you want your beads to be. You will need to make around 30 beads.

Step 2 Take a cocktail stick and wrap one of the pieces of paper around it in a tight coil.

Step 3 Cover the paper you have rolled around the stick with paste.

Step 4 Once the paper is all covered in paste, push it down the cocktail stick and wrap another piece of paper around the top of the stick. Cover that in paste as well. Keep doing this until the stick is full.

Step 5 Once the stick is full, start making new beads on a new cocktail stick, until you have between 20 – 30 beads.

Step 6 Wait until all the beads are dry, then remove them from the cocktail sticks.

Step 7 Paint and decorate the beads using your colour paints and glitter. You could choose a combination of your favourite colours – or for a totally Miley look, why not combine hot pink with some funky purple glitter? Seal with a coat of the clear nail varnish.

Step 8 Wait until the paint is dry, then thread the beads onto your string. If you want to, you could tie a knot in the string between each bead, to stop them sliding around. Ask an adult to help you if you find this part tricky.

Step 9 Voila! Put on your awesome Miley glitter necklace and show all your friends and family what an amazing and unique accessory you have made!

Hannah Montana Co-stars

Emily Osment

AKA: Lilly Truscott

Friends

Facts **Info** **Extras**

Lilly Truscott is the best friend of Miley Stewart and Oliver Oken. She is a huge Hannah Montana fan, she was even one before she found out Miley's secret. Lilly attends Hannah Montana events with Hannah in disguise, using the alias "Lola". Lilly loves skateboarding and surfing. She also loves cute clothes and boys, although she is a very tomboy-ish character.

In real life too, Emily and Miley are great friends! Miley once taught Emily to play the guitar, in exchange for Emily giving her knitting lessons.

Mitchel Musso

AKA: Oliver Oken

Friends

Facts   Info   Extras

Oliver and Lilly Truscott have been best friends since pre-school, and he has been friends with Miley Stewart since she moved to California. Initially, Oliver was in love with Hannah Montana; however, this ended after he learned that Hannah was really Miley.

Off-set, Mitchel, Emily and Miley are really close, always texting each other when they're not hanging out on set. Mitchel loves making music, and one day he sees himself on-stage, playing to stadiums around the world.

'My favourite thing the show has given me is the fans. I love having fans! That's my favourite thing, for people to come up and ask for an autograph. It's all about them and they're there for you!'

Jason Earles

AKA: Jackson Stewart

Friends

Facts | Info | Extras

Jackson Stewart is Miley's teenage brother. According to Robbie Ray's yelling, Jackson's full name is Jackson Rod Stewart, named after the singer Rod Stewart. Jackson is the dorky and slightly geeky older brother to Miley, laid back and casual, who would rather be silly than be serious. Jackson works at Rico's Surf Shop on the beach.

Jason Earles has become really close to the real Cyrus family since working on Hannah Montana – he often jokes that he should change his name to Jason Ray Cyrus! What many people don't know is that Jason is actually a trained Shakespearean actor. Who'd have thought that!

'The whole cast is just as close off-set as on it. We're always looking for reasons to hang out together, like maybe we'll go grab sushi together, or go watch a movie.'

Billy Ray Cyrus

AKA: Robbie Ray Stewart

Friends

Facts   Info   Extras

Robbie Ray Stewart is Miley Stewart's father – and the character is loosely based on Miley's real life pop, Billy Ray. Robbie is a widower and father of Jackson and Miley. He gave up his career as the famous singer Robbie Ray so he could take care of his children after his wife died. He is Hannah Montana's dad and manager/producer, and he writes most of Hannah's songs. When he is Hannah's manager, he wears a moustache to disguise his identity.

Which HANNAH MONTANA star are you?

If you were in Hannah Montana, who do you think you would be most like? Take the test and find out!

1 The sun is out and the weekend is coming up – what do you want to do?
- a) Grab your guitar and head to the beach
- b) Hole-in-one – play golf any day!
- c) Go to the skatepark with friends
- d) Chill out on the sofa
- e) Beach with mates
- f) Pony-trekking

2 What do you look for in your ideal partner?
- a) Elegance
- b) Honesty
- c) Someone who can sing songs to me
- d) Someone who can bust a groove on the dance floor
- e) Humour
- f) Down-to-earth nature and independence

3 When it comes to school, what do you think?
- a) Celebrate your uniqueness and go for your goals
- b) Do your homework – it will pay off!
- c) Be yourself – you don't have to follow the cool gang
- d) Suck up to your teachers!
- e) Work hard and play hard
- f) Hard work is the key

4 Who is your celebrity idol?
- a) John Wayne
- b) Audrey Hepburn
- c) Keanu Reeves
- d) Richard Branagh
- e) Leonardo DiCaprio
- f) Hilary Duff

5 If you go out on a hot date, what food would you like?
- a) Ribs and wings!
- b) Chinese
- c) As long as there's ice cream, I'm not fussy!
- d) Mexican
- e) Pizza
- f) Sushi

So, what answer did you give most?
Mostly As: The loveable rogue – Billy Ray
Mostly Bs: Emily Osment – lucky you!
Mostly Cs: You like to goof around like Mitchell Musso
Mostly Ds: You're funny, just like Jason Earles
Mostly Es: You're brilliant, just like Cody Linley
Mostly Fs: You're like Miley – honest and gorgeous

Fame Calling!

1 *If you went to a talent show, you would…*
- a) sing
- b) dance
- c) act
- d) tell jokes

2 *You dream of…*
- a) having a platinum album
- b) dancing on Broadway
- c) winning an Oscar
- d) hosting your own chat show

3 *Your friends would describe you as…*
- a) a musical genius
- b) twinkle toes
- c) just so dramatic, darling!
- d) always laughing and talking in class

Mostly As – Start practicing your scales, you are a born performer and your musical talent will make you a star!

Mostly Bs – You would dance all day if you could! Keep it up and you'll be dancing your way to the top!

Mostly Cs – Well, look at you, you'll be centre-stage in no time. You were born to act and really come alive when you are in front of the camera!

Mostly Ds – You love to entertain and are interested in other people. You should be great on TV.

Tennessee Banana Split

If she's ever fixing a pudding for her family or friends, Miley loves to make this totally tasty Tennessee Banana Split. It's super easy to make, and absolutely delicious! Make sure you get an adult to help you make the chocolate sauce as it's easy to burn yourself – and Miley is all about safety first, especially in the kitchen.

For the banana split:

2 bananas

1 can whipped cream

1 tub vanilla ice cream

1 chocolate-coated
   honeycomb bar, crushed

30g/1oz chocolate coated
peanut sweets

For the chocolate sauce:

110g/4oz dark chocolate

2 tbsp golden syrup

75ml/2fl oz water

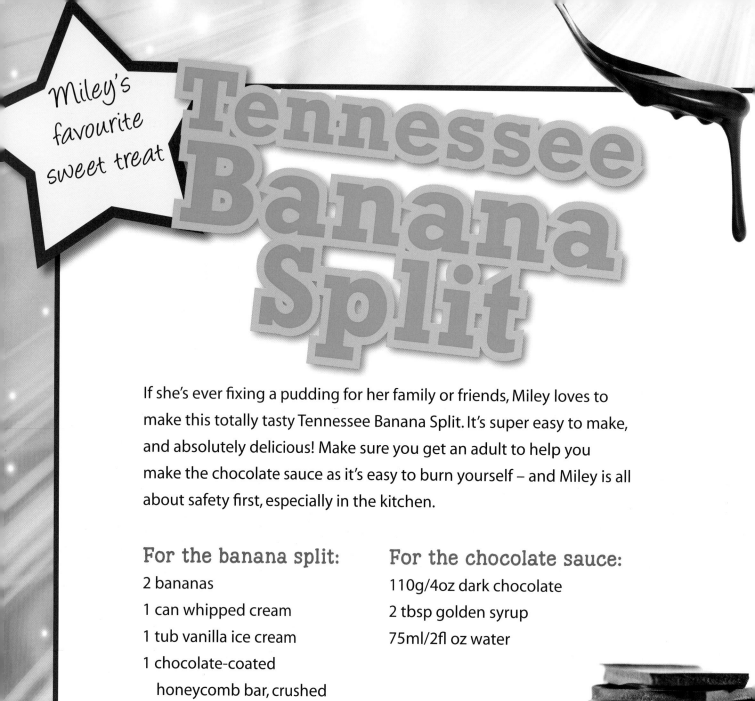

Step 1 Prepare the chocolate sauce by melting the chocolate with the syrup and water in a small pan over a low heat. You need to keep stirring until the chocolate has all melted then take the pan off the heat. Make sure you keep the heat low, as this mixture can burn easily.

Step 2 Peel your bananas and cut them in half, longways. Put them on the dish you're going to serve them in.

Step 3 Spoon out some ice cream and put it in between your banana, in the middle. Then squirt over some of your squirty cream.

Step 4 Carefully pour over the chocolate sauce from the pan.

Step 5 Take a handful of the crushed honeycomb bar and chocolate coated peanut sweets, and sprinkle them over your banana.

Step 6 Serve your delicious Tennessee Banana Split up to your friends or family – but make sure you get some, it'll go quickly!

Music

With dad Billy Ray Cyrus who is a singing legend in his own right, and a godmother who is the all time queen of country, Dolly Parton, it seems inevitable that this bubbly brunette was going to be a musical talent. In fact, her parents often say she could sing before she could speak – she was always humming away to herself as a small child. Winning the starring role on *Hannah Montana* gave Miley a real chance to showcase her talents.

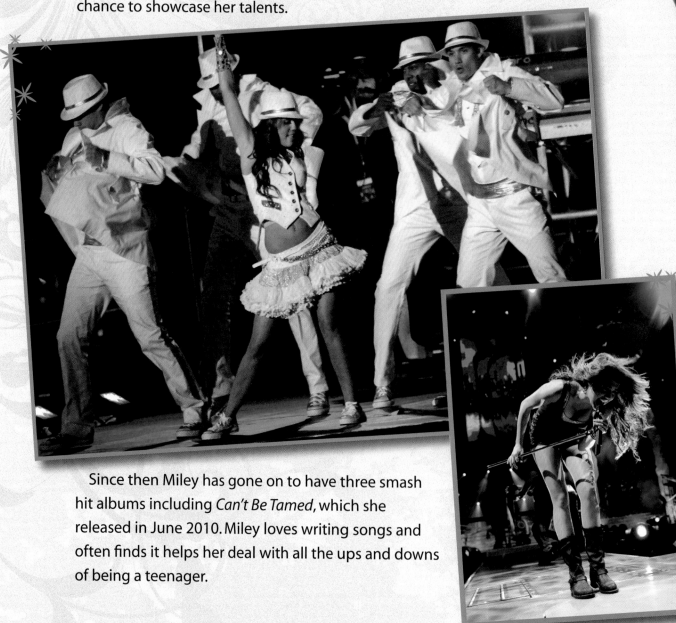

Since then Miley has gone on to have three smash hit albums including *Can't Be Tamed*, which she released in June 2010. Miley loves writing songs and often finds it helps her deal with all the ups and downs of being a teenager.

Songwriting is what I really want to do with my life forever

29

Touring

The success of the *Hannah Montana* series soon led to Miley leaving her home of California and embarking on the Best of Both Worlds tour around America. The teen queen played sold-out stadiums to thousands of fans, putting on an explosive performance, night after night. Where does she get her energy from?! Once she'd proven to herself and all her fans that she really was born to be on the stage, there was no stopping her.

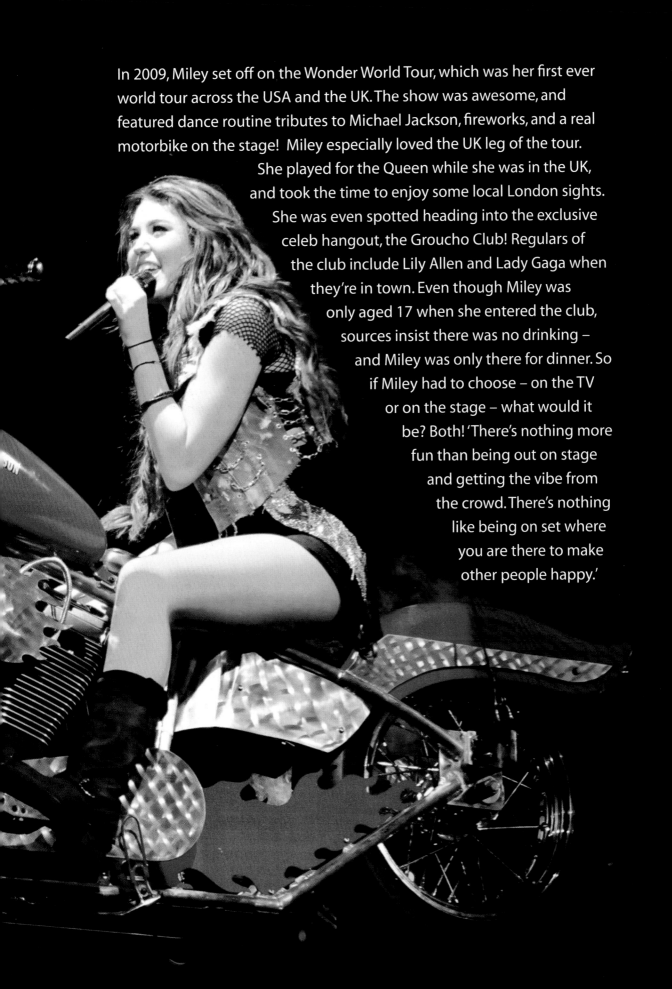

In 2009, Miley set off on the Wonder World Tour, which was her first ever world tour across the USA and the UK. The show was awesome, and featured dance routine tributes to Michael Jackson, fireworks, and a real motorbike on the stage! Miley especially loved the UK leg of the tour. She played for the Queen while she was in the UK, and took the time to enjoy some local London sights. She was even spotted heading into the exclusive celeb hangout, the Groucho Club! Regulars of the club include Lily Allen and Lady Gaga when they're in town. Even though Miley was only aged 17 when she entered the club, sources insist there was no drinking – and Miley was only there for dinner. So if Miley had to choose – on the TV or on the stage – what would it be? Both! 'There's nothing more fun than being out on stage and getting the vibe from the crowd. There's nothing like being on set where you are there to make other people happy.'

Changing her sound

Even though the teen queen started out playing pop, she's hinted that she might be looking to change her musical style to a more edgy sound. 'I want to do my last pop record,' Miley said in 2009. 'I kinda want this to be my last record for a little while and be able to take a break and just get all the types of music that I really love … you know my favourite styles … Because in a few years, as I grow up, so will my fans and I won't have to focus on that as much and I'll be able to have more of the sound of music that I'm into.' And we are loving Miley's latest album, *Can't Be Tamed*. It totally rocks! And the first single went straight into top 10s across the world, there's no stopping her!

Who is one of Miley's mentors?

See p.46 for the goss code!

Miley's Ultimate Idol?

It's SASHA FIERCE!

Miley – 'I want to be like Beyonce. She is the ultimate woman. You look at her and you don't think, "I wonder what her personal life is like." You look at her and you go, "That girl on the stage is a superstar." You don't care about anything else; you only care about her music. So I would hope that would be me in the future.'

Miley's Playlist

Hilary Duff

Kelly Clarkson

Ashlee Simpson

Elvis Presley

John Mayer

The Killers

Coldplay

Shania Twain

Rob Thomas

John Lennon

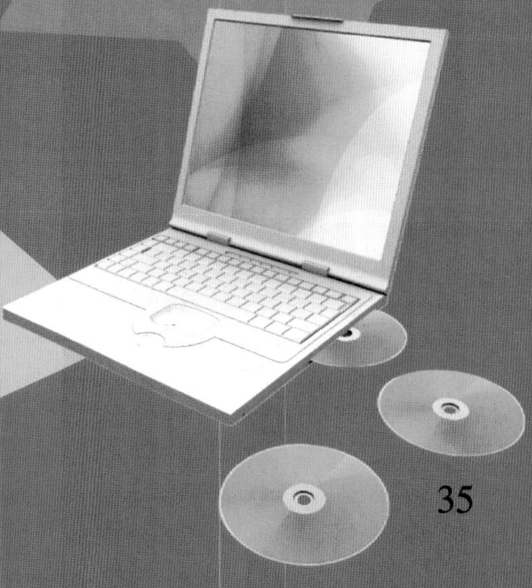

The Ultimate Miley Sleepover!

Miley loves spending time with her friends, and what better way to get some real bonding in than to invite all your bestest buds over for a sleepover? If you want to throw the ultimate Miley sleepover, just follow these steps.

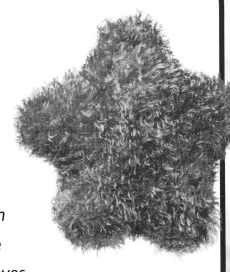

You will need

- Your **best friends**
- Some tasty **sleepover treats** (try making the Tennessee Banana Split). Miley also loves cookie dough and cashews for munching with her buds.
- Some fun **movies** to watch. For the ultimate Miley experience, make sure you have *Bolt*, and definitely *High School Musical*, which is one of Miley's all-time favourite films that she loves to watch with her sisters. She also loves watching *Laguna Beach* and *The Suite Life of Zack & Cody*
- Some **face-masks**, for ultimate girly pampering
- **Scented candles** – Miley's favourite scent is vanilla
- Colourful **nail varnish**
- Some **funky music** – you'll probably want Beyonce, Rihanna, Lady Gaga, John Mayer or Kelly Clarkson!

Kick off the party by putting on your favourite songs and making the banana splits – yum! Next up, manicure! Wash your hands and file each other's nails so they match the shape of the bottom of your nail. Then for the fun part, pick your favourite nail colour and apply two coats. For a really funky look, why not paint alternate fingers different colours! While you are waiting for your nails to dry, you could record your own cool tv show on your phone, just like Miley and Mandi. Finally, ask an adult to light the scented candles, pamper yourself with your face-mask and kick back to your favourite film. Awesome!

Friends & Fashion

Miley's BFFs

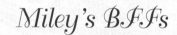

Miley's friends have always been super important to her. Emily Osment and Miley are BFFs – the two of them are always texting each other and chatting online. But friendship didn't always come so easily. When they first met, the pair were from completely different worlds and they just didn't seem to have anything in common. But that's all history now, as Miley says, 'For all our troubles, deep down I know we loved each other, even then.' Miley's other famous pals include Brenda Song, Ashley Tisdale, Taylor Swift and Demi Lovato!

Miley and Demi

The media had reported rumours of a feud between the two girls for years, but in fact, nothing could be further from the truth. Miley even posted a pic of the two Disney buds on her Twitter with a message that read *that's true friendship.'* And Miley and boyfriend Liam have even been seen at trendy Beverly Hills hangouts with Demi.

Miley and Mandy

While on tour, Miley met BFF Mandy Jiroux, her backing dancer, and in February 2008 the two girls have a YouTube channel, called MileyMandy, which they update with new videos of their show called *The Miley and Mandy Show*. The girls film the show themselves and edit it too – how cool is that?! In early 2010, the girls were really busy, Miley was working on HM4 and Mandy on BeachGirl5 so they haven't had much time to post new vids – fingers crossed they'll be back!

Miley's Horoscope

Miley is a positive and energetic Sagittarius. Sagittarians are renowned for their honesty, but Miley might want to remember to keep some things to herself, as she's in danger of being more honest than some sensitive souls can handle! Sagittarians are also known for being fun and light-hearted, which Miley certainly is! However, they're also known for being fiercely independent, so although Miley knows her dad will always be there in the background if she needs him, she's perfectly capable of looking after herself, but we already knew that! Finally, Sagittarians are fearless natural born performers who love travelling, all of which spells out many more amazing world tours and fantastic performances from this megastar!

Miley's love life over the past few exciting years has kept us all hooked so is Liam destined to be The One? Only the stars hold the key to Miley's heart!

Past love Nick Jonas of the Jonas Brothers is a wise and reliable Virgo. While Virgos are worlds away from Miley's Sagittarius in character, these two signs balance each other out perfectly. Nick kept her grounded when everything around her was crazy. However, ever the Sagittarian, Miley craves freedom and may have felt unable to fully spread her wings. Perhaps as she grows up, she'll want the security that Nick has to offer a whole lot more. Only time will tell!

Model, musician and life-loving Leo, Justin Gaston, is another lucky man to have had romantic ties to Miley. With both being such headstrong star signs, this was bound to an exciting, if short-lived, match! Leos are naturally warm, generous and bursting with charisma. But it may have been a case of 'this town ain't big enough for the both of us' that led to the spilt.

Current beau, the swoonable Liam Hemsworth, is an ambitious and patient Capricorn, with many of the qualities of former boyfriend, Nick. Miley finds Liam's Capricornian depth and mystery intriguing, he finds her bubbliness fascinating, and he's a great listener, giving her all the reassurance she needs now to make the next steps in her acting career. Capricorns are naturally loyal so it's unlikely Liam will be breaking Miley's heart any time soon …

What is Miley's favourite book?

See p.46 for the goss code!

Miley's fashion sense

When it comes to style, Miley knows what she likes – and this is one sassy teen who's not afraid to wear anything! Whether she's putting on a ballgown for the Oscars or grabbing a coffee with her BFFs, she is always looking her best. And she's regularly spotted wearing the coolest threads on red carpets across the world – from designers like Valentino, Hervé Léger, Moschino, and more!

Chilled Miley

But Miley's not afraid to dress down when she's just hanging out at home or with her friends, and can often be seen in jeans with UGG boots and cute tees. 'I think from having to dress up on Hannah Montana, on my days off or in the studio I like being as comfy as possible. My style is very comfy casual. Sometimes I like to put on jeans, a white t-shirt and cute boots and sometimes I like being in little Juicy sweats – it depends on my mood.'

Accessories Girls!

Miley loves her accessories and is rarely seen without a clutch or a bangle: 'I always have two bracelets on my arm …you'll never see me without them ever!' Little touches like these can really bring an old outfit back to life and can transform a daytime look into something extra special for a party in the evening!

Red Carpet Miley

When there is a red carpet in sight, Miley is always the most glamorous person around – the cameras could click at any moment! Miley likes to wear elegant dresses, often in red, black or white, with matching shoes. Simple but stunning.

Colour Me Beautiful

Miley always knows what colours suit her best and that is why her clothes so often look like they were made for her. And Miley also knows that the colours we wear have a big effect on the way we feel and the way people see us. Do you know which colours suit you best? Try this simple test to find out! Hold two pieces of jewellery – one gold coloured and one silver coloured piece – up against your skin, and look in the mirror. Which looks brighter on your skin? One will jump out on you more than the other.

If gold looks brighter:
You suit gorgeous rich, warm colours. Try yellows, oranges, browns, reds and purples. In general, blues and greens aren't the best colours for you, but if you do go for them, make sure they are bright and bold shades, not pastel colours.

If silver looks brighter:
Cooler colours suit you perfectly. Try blues, green, greys and violets. Light shades will really complement your skin tone too. In general it is best to steer clear of reds and oranges, as they'll wash you out.

Hair Flair

These are going to be the hairstyles of 2011 and Miley is sure to be rocking some of them so why not try them yourself?

The classic up do

Sometimes a bit of red carpet glamour is called for and Miley loves to put her hair up for the occasion. Here's how you do it! Pull your hair back into a ponytail, slightly to the left, and twist it. Twist your ponytail in a clockwise direction twice. With your left hand, hold the base of the ponytail and with your right hand, hold its end up (pointing towards the ceiling). Bend the tail of your ponytail and use your left hand to hide it and tuck the end of your ponytail under the roll. Secure with hair grips. Accessorise with jewelled clips and slides and you're ready for the big entrance!

Accessories

Miley loves hair accessories like scarves, hats and diamante grips. They look stylish and are perfect for day and night. Feather hairbands are going to be huge in 2011 so be ahead of the trend!

Beach beautiful

This is one for the long summer days. Pull hair back loosely into a low ponytail. Twist around as if making a bun then tie gently into a knot and fasten with hair grips. Pull your fringe gently to the side, letting it fall over your forehead slightly and fix with a pretty grip or flower. Finish with spray and you're hot to trot!

The quiff

Hold the front section of your hair across your forehead (about 4cm back from your hairline will do.) Get a comb and, starting at the ends of your hair, carefully brush back towards your head. This is called backcombing and will keep your quiff looking super smart! Spray with hairspray and using grips carefully pin the ends of your hair to the top of your head. Finish with a side-pony and you'll be the funkiest girl in school!

Tip: Remember, your hair is easier to style if it isn't freshly washed.

Secret Codecracker

Do you know all the latest Miley gossip? Use the goss code below to crack these secret messages! Each letter has been replaced by a symbol but remember, once you've worked it out, don't tell anyone – it's a secret! You can even use the symbols to write your own private messages to your BFFs!

What is Miley's motto?

What is Hannah Montana's favourite colour?

What is Miley's favourite song?

❀	A	●	F	🎁	K	✋	Q	🐦	V
☕	B	🎂	G	☼	L	✂	R	🍭	W
✋	C	♪	H	✈	M	⊙	S	🎻	X
✋	D	★	I	◐	N	⚡	T	〰	Y
🌸	E	🍃	J	✉	O	☎	U	🔥	Z
				👁	P				

What's your superstar style – HANNAH or MILEY?

Miley is a real trend-setter and rocks loads of different looks, and her popstar alter-ego Hannah Montana is a real girly girl, but what about you? Is your style more Miley, Hannah or do you set your own trends?

1 How do you like your hair?
- a) blond and straight
- b) brunette and wavy
- c) something unique –
  C.

2 What do you think about make-up
- a) lots of eyeshadow and glitter
- b) just a touch - I like the natural look
- c)

3 Your wardrobe is
- a) big enough to throw a party in
- b) small but tasteful and elegant
- c) totally cool –

4 Your style in one word
- a) glamour
- b) sophisticated
- c) _____

5 I never leave the house without
- a) lip gloss
- b) my bangles
- c) _____

Mostly As:
You're totally Hannah!
Mostly Bs:
Miley's your style soulmate
Mostly Cs:
You are a style icon – work it girl!

Factfile

Every girl has a popstar hiding inside her. For Miley, her alter ego is Hannah! But what about you? Fill in the two factfiles below, one which is for the everyday you – and then invent some cool details for your popstar alter ego!

EVERYDAY YOU

Name: Megan

Hair colour: Blonde

Eye colour: Blue

Style: Tomboy X Girly Girl

Favourite outfit: Black dress

Favourite t-shirt colour: Purple

Skirt or jeans? Bath

What kind of phone do you use? Iphone

Shoes highs or lows? high

Sunglasses or hairclips? Hairclips

Pets: Dn3c 3fpbra4r

Where do you live?: Fife

What car do you drive?: Red

Who are your BFFS? Shaz Sarah

Where's your favourite place to shop? Pets at home

Who's your ideal guy?

What's your ideal holiday? on a beach

48

And be creative. Even if you always wear flats and would never dye your hair – your popstar alter ego can do anything! If you want your popstar to have purple hair and wear towering platforms – then go right ahead. If you're preppy, your popstar could be totally punky. Anything is possible – just ask Miley!

POPSTAR YOU

Name: ....

Hair colour: ....

Eye colour: ....

Style: ....

Favourite outfit: ....

Favourite t-shirt colour: ....

Skirt or jeans? ....

What kind of phone do you use? ....

Shoes highs or lows? ....

Sunglasses or hairclips? ....

Pets: ....

Where do you live?: ....

What car do you drive?: ....

Who are your BFFS? ....

Where's your favourite place to shop?
....

Who's your ideal guy? ....

What's your ideal holiday? ....
....

The Miley Quiz

1 What is Miley's real name?
- a) Brandi Cyrus
- b) Smiley Cyrus
- c) Destiny Hope Cyrus
- d) Billy Ray Cyrus

2 Who is Miley's ultimate idol?
- a) Kelly Clarkson
- b) Beyonce
- c) Britney Spears
- d) Shakira

3 What is Miley's worst bad habit?
- a) Biting her nails
- b) Finishing other people's sentences
- c) Talking with her mouth full
- d) Picking her nose!

4 Where is Miley from?
- a) Tennessee
- b) Alabama
- c) California
- d) New York

5 What is Miley's favourite sport?
- a) Cheerleading
- b) Baseball
- c) Gymnastics
- d) Football

6 What is Miley's favourite hobby?
- a) Hanging out with friends
- b) Going shopping!
- c) Texting on her BlackBerry
- d) Watching Zac and Cody

7 What is Miley's favourite season?
- a) Summer
- b) Winter
- c) Spring
- d) Autumn

8 Who plays Hannah Montana's dad in the show?
- a) Johnny Depp
- b) Billy Ray Cyrus
- c) Jesse McCartney
- d) Leonardo DiCaprio

9 Who does Miley co-host her YouTube show with?
- a) Mandy
- b) Molly
- c) Mindy
- d) Mary

10 **How does Miley like to dazzle on the red carpet?**
- a) Jewellery, and lots of it. It's all about the bling!
- b) Killer heels
- c) A rock-star dress!
- d) A handbag by her favourite designer, Zuhair

11 **What movie does Miley like to watch over and over?**
- a) Steel Magnolias
- b) Fame
- c) High School Musical
- d) Camp Rock

12 **When Miley has her girls over for a sleepover, what does she love to make for them?**
- a) Tennessee Banana Split
- b) Popcorn
- c) Snickers bar
- d) Gummy bears

13 **What is the name of Miley's smash hit single?**
- a) Achy Breaky Heart
- b) The Climb
- c) Reach for the Stars
- d) Breaking Free

14 **What is Miley's favourite fashion statement?**
- a) Punky armwarmers
- b) Glitter eyeshadow
- c) Rock-chick nails
- d) A sparkly scarf

15 **How does Miley like to start the day off?**
- a) A bowl of oatmeal with two scoops of ice-cream
- b) A slice of toast
- c) Fresh fruit and yoghurt
- d) A big bowl of lucky charms

16 **When Miley isn't playing Hannah, what does she like to wear?**
- a) A cute tee, jeans and UGG boots
- b) Sweats and sneakers
- c) Anything pink!
- d) The same outfits as Hannah

17 **What is Miley's new movie called?**
- a) Song and Dance
- b) Save the Last Dance
- c) The Last Song
- d) The First Song

18 **Who are Hannah Montana's BFF's?**
- a) Oliver and Lilly
- b) Zac and Cody
- c) Demi and Selena
- d) Zac and Vanessa

Love

Since becoming a teenager, Miley has hardly had a conventional upbringing – the long hours she had to work on the *Hannah Montana* set meant that boyfriends weren't top of her priorities. Dad Billy Ray didn't mind that, after all, what daddy wants to have to face the truth that his little girl is grown up? But reality is that Miley's lovelife is constantly in the spotlight.

Since reaching her mid teens, Miley has been linked to a whole string of famous hotties, most notably the gorgeous Jonas brother, Nick. Although they tried to keep quiet about their relationship, the paparazzi soon found them out, and they were pictured together everywhere. Miley was deliriously happy with Nick – both were into music, and would spend evenings sharing songs on their guitars. But perhaps they were just too similar because after a year and a half, the pair called it quits in late 2007.

Miley was distraught. Soon after breaking up with Nick, she dyed her hair black in an effort to rebel against everything she'd had with Nick. But luckily it didn't take too long for Miley to bounce back.

Even though Miley's lovelife is important to her, she's still knows that in the end, her girlfriends are those who will stick by her, no matter what. 'Girlfriends are forever,' she says. 'You always need to remember that and cherish your special friendships.'

It wasn't too long before Miley was in demand and feeling confident about herself as well she should! In 2009, while on the set of movie *The Last Song*, she developed a close friendship with co-star Liam Hemsworth, an Aussie actor who also just happens to be totally hot!!

Miley even spent New Year 2009 in Australia with Liam's friends and family – could it be love?! Read on to find out more!

'I've never gotten along with someone so well,' Miley says about her latest boyf. *'I was a little anxious about making this movie; I wanted everything to be perfect. To go on set and feel insecure was a totally new element for me. But he felt the same way. He admitted his insecurities, and it was really nice to have someone who understands me for once.'*

Trying to keep their friendship private, Miley even went so far as to delete her Twitter! 'It sucks when your personal life becomes public,' she explains. 'So I'm finding ways to make my personal and private life more of my life – which is one of the reasons why I deleted my Twitter. We've decided that any type of relationship that we have, we will always just keep it very D.L. First and foremost, we are best friends, so that's what I tell people all the time.' Miley admits that Liam is always there for her and always kept her confidence up whilst filming.

Even though they're in the spotlight all the time, Miley was reluctant to confirm whether they are officially dating or not, one thing is for sure, they look great together. Miley and Liam do normal-couple things all the time – they love going on date nights, and can often be spotted grabbing coffee and sushi around West Hollywood.

CROSSWORD

Across
2. One of Miley's favourite films
3. Lilly Truscott's alias in *Hannah Montana*
4. Miley's favourite scented candle
7. Number of dogs Miley owns
8. Where the show *Hannah Montana* is set
9. State Miley was born in

Down
1. Country legend and Miley's godmother
2. Miley's dad's name
5. Miley's musical idol
6. Miley's favourite season

What is Miley's favourite film?

⊙ ⁖ ✿ ✿ ☺
✈ ✿ 🎂 ⚫ ✉ ⚙ ★ ✿ ⊙

See p.46 for the goss code!

WORDSEARCH

Search for the words listed below in the grid.

```
R A B A Y E L I M E H S E E D L O B
I O W E B S T R E D S A L G D I U T
M U C A N F E D K I T A Y I A L O H
N D Y K A S D R A T S P O P F L E M
B I R M C N O A J O A Z R E S Y N I
E T U E A H R T G Z P D E O Y O G H
H I S A G F I N A S G C J F D U L A
J O G R A E N C Q D O Y C A B S W N
Y N O J Y F O S K Q M A F A S R I N
T S E D A O L F N S G R N O A H J A
D A R A S F P C F A A Y I Z S E H H
C T O L I V E R E M I L S I D I A E
O J B O D N R A N U Q L G L I T T M
L H B H O G F U M O Z I K D H A K O
G I I S T H E C L I M B S A E M S R
O Q E J A N N D I E C E S E R D I P
S X S A T N G L A M E G I A Z J C A
A C D I O R M O N T A N A G S N Z O
```

Hidden Words:

THE CLIMB	HANNAH	MONTANA
MILEY	CYRUS	JAKE
OLIVER	BILLY RAY	ROBBIE
LILLY	ROCK CHICK	POPSTAR

ANSWERS

page 56 Miley Crossword

1. Dolly Parton
2a. Bolt
2d. Billy Ray
3. Lola
4. Vanilla
5. Beyonce
6. Summer
7. Four
8. Malibu
9. Tennessee

page 50 Miley Quiz

1. Destiny Hope Cyrus
2. Beyonce
3. Biting her nails
4. Tennessee
5. Cheerleading
6. Going shopping!
7. Summer
8. Billy Ray Cyrus
9. Mandy
10. Jewellery
11. Steel Magnolias
12. Pretty li'l peppermint creams
13. The Climb
14. Punky armwarmers
15. A bowl of oatmeal with two scoops of ice-cream
16. A cute tee, jeans and UGG boots
17. The Last Song
18. Oliver and Lilly

page 59 Wordsearch

```
R A B A Y E L I M E H S E E D L O B
I O W E B S T R E D S A L G D I U T
M U C A N F E D K I T A Y I A L O H
N D Y K A S D R A T S P O P F L E M
B I R M C N O A J O A Z R E S Y N I
E T U E A H R T G Z P D E O Y O G H
H I S A G F I N A S G C J F D U L A
J O G R A E N C Q D O Y C A B S W N
Y N O J Y F O S K Q M A F A S R I N
T S E D A O L F N S G R N O A H J A
D A R A S F P C F A A Y I Z S E H H
C T O L I V E R E M I L S I D I A E
O J B O D N R A N U Q L G L I T T M
L H B H O G F U M O Z I K D H A K O
G I I S T H E C L I M B S A E M S R
O Q E J A N N D I E C E S E R D I P
S X S A T N G L A M E G I A Z J C A
A C D I O R M O N T A N A G S N Z O
```

Picture Credits

All pictures courtesy of Getty Images.

Acknowledgements

Posy Edwards would like to thank Helia Phoenix, Jane Sturrock, Nicola Crossley, Helen Ewing, James Martindale, Rich Carr and Louise Millar

Copyright © Posy Edwards 2010

The right of Posy Edwards to be identified as
the author of this work has been asserted in accordance with the
Copyright, Designs and Patents Act 1988.

First published in hardback in Great Britain in 2010 by
Orion Books an imprint of the Orion Publishing Group Ltd
Orion House, 5 Upper St Martin's Lane, London WC2H 9EA
An Hachette UK Company

10 9 8 7 6 5 4 3 2 1

A CIP catalogue record for this book is available from the British Library.

ISBN: 978 1 409 11497 0

Designed by Louise Millar
Printed in Spain by Cayfosa

The Orion Publishing Group's policy is to use papers that are natural, renewable and recyclable and made from wood grown in sustainable forests. The logging and manufacturing processes are expected to conform to the environmental regulations of the country of origin.

Every effort has been made to fulfil requirements with regard to reproducing copyright material. The author and publisher will be glad to rectify any omissions at the earliest opportunity.

www.orionbooks.co.uk